A Note from
Mary Pope Osborne About the

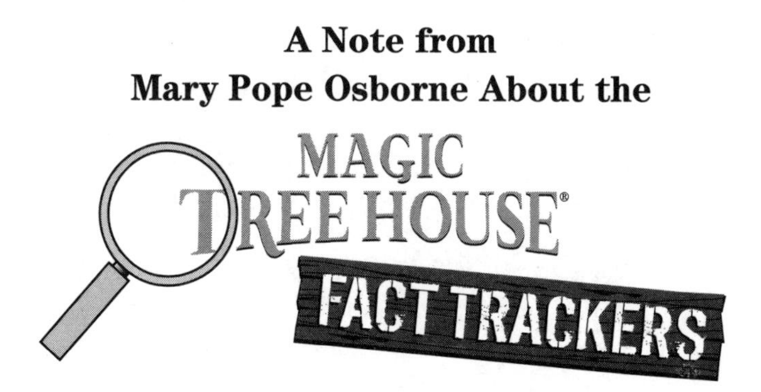

When I write Magic Tree House® adventures, I love including facts about the times and places Jack and Annie visit. But when readers finish these adventures, I want them to learn even more. So that's why we write a series of nonfiction books that are companions to the fiction titles in the Magic Tree House® series. We call these books Fact Trackers because we love to track the facts! Whether we're researching dinosaurs, pyramids, Pilgrims, sea monsters, or cobras, we're always amazed at how wondrous and surprising the real world is. We want you to experience the same wonder we do—so get out your pencils and notebooks and hit the trail with us. You can be a Magic Tree House® Fact Tracker, too!

Mary Pope Osborne

Here's what kids, parents, and teachers have to say about the Magic Tree House® Fact Trackers:

"They are so good. I can't wait for the next one. All I can say for now is prepare to be amazed!" —Alexander N.

"I have read every Magic Tree House book there is. The [Fact Trackers] are a thrilling way to get more information about the special events in the story." —John R.

"These are fascinating nonfiction books that enhance the magical time-traveling adventures of Jack and Annie. I love these books, especially *American Revolution.* I was learning so much, and I didn't even know it!" —Tori Beth S.

"[They] are an excellent 'behind-the-scenes' look at what the [Magic Tree House fiction] has started in your imagination! You can't buy one without the other; they are such a complement to one another." —Erika N., mom

"Magic Tree House [Fact Trackers] took my children on a journey from Frog Creek, Pennsylvania, to so many significant historical events! The detailed manuals are a remarkable addition to the classic fiction Magic Tree House books we adore!" —Jenny S., mom

"[They] are very useful tools in my classroom, as they allow for students to be part of the planning process. Together, we find facts in the [Fact Trackers] to extend the learning introduced in the fictional companions. Researching and planning classroom activities, such as our class Olympics based on facts found in *Ancient Greece and the Olympics*, help create a genuine love for learning!" —Paula H., teacher

Dog Heroes

A NONFICTION COMPANION TO MAGIC TREE HOUSE MERLIN MISSION #18:

Dogs in the Dead of Night

BY MARY POPE OSBORNE
AND NATALIE POPE BOYCE

ILLUSTRATED BY SAL MURDOCCA

A STEPPING STONE BOOK™
Random House New York

The Magic Tree House Fact Tracker series was formerly known as the Magic Tree House Research Guide series. Magic Tree House Merlin Mission #18 was formerly known as Magic Tree House #46.

Visit us on the Web!
SteppingStonesBooks.com
MagicTreeHouse.com

Educators and librarians, for a variety of teaching tools, visit us at
RHTeachersLibrarians.com

Library of Congress Cataloging-in-Publication Data
Osborne, Mary Pope.
Dog heroes / by Mary Pope Osborne and Natalie Pope Boyce ;
illustrated by Sal Murdocca.
p. cm. — (Magic tree house fact tracker)
"A Stepping Stone book."
Includes index.
ISBN 978-0-375-86012-6 (trade) — ISBN 978-0-375-96012-3 (lib. bdg.) —
ISBN 978-0-307-97554-6 (ebook)
1. Dogs—Juvenile literature. 2. Animal heroes—Juvenile literature.
3. Working dogs—Juvenile literature. I. Boyce, Natalie Pope.
II. Murdocca, Sal, ill. III. Title.
SF426.5.O83 2011 636.7—dc22 2010046114

Printed in the United States of America
22 21

This book has been officially leveled by using the F&P Text Level Gradient™ Leveling System.

In celebration of Nan, Barney, Gulley, Isaac, Shy Dog, Raquel, Teddy, Bailey, Merlin, Lula, Mr. Bezo, Joey, Little Bear, Pearl, Boola, Louie, Jasper, Maudie, Baby, Monty, Westy, Annie, Busby, Nicky, and Chilko

Scientific Consultant:

STANLEY COREN, Ph.D., F.R.S.C., Professor Emeritus, Department of Psychology, University of British Columbia

Education Consultant:

HEIDI JOHNSON, Earth Science and Paleontology, Lowell Junior High School, Bisbee, Arizona

Very special thanks to the Random House team who make it all worthwhile: Gloria Cheng; Mallory Loehr; Chelsea Eberly, our fantastic photo researcher; Sal Murdocca, our superb artist; and as always to our editor, the intrepid Diane Landolf

DOG HEROES

Contents

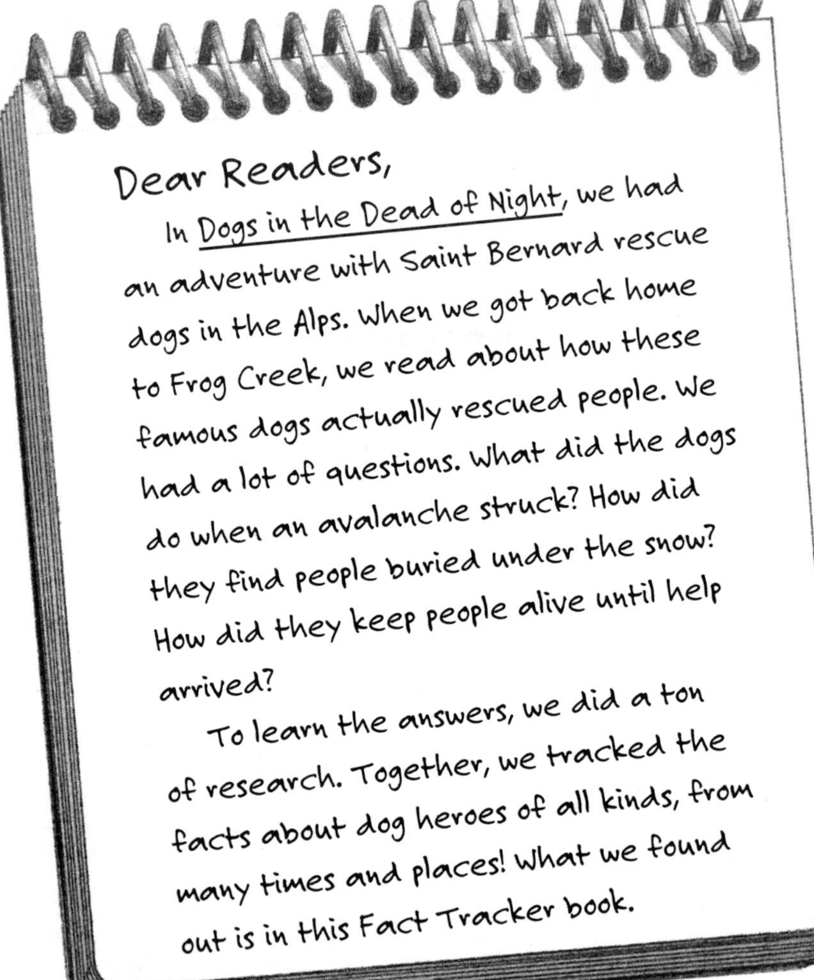

Dear Readers,

In Dogs in the Dead of Night, we had an adventure with Saint Bernard rescue dogs in the Alps. When we got back home to Frog Creek, we read about how these famous dogs actually rescued people. We had a lot of questions. What did the dogs do when an avalanche struck? How did they find people buried under the snow? How did they keep people alive until help arrived?

To learn the answers, we did a ton of research. Together, we tracked the facts about dog heroes of all kinds, from many times and places! What we found out is in this Fact Tracker book.

We learned that dogs and people have been together for thousands of years. We also learned that dogs have a powerful sense of smell that helps them find people. Dogs sniff a trail to track a scent. We are a little like that—but we track facts! Instead of sniffing a trail, we research in books and on the Internet. So get your notebooks, get your backpack, and come be a fact tracker with us!

Jack

Annie

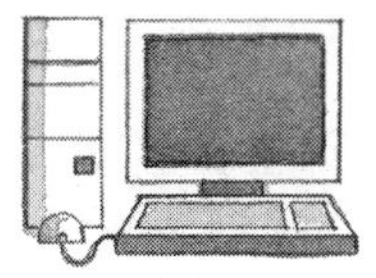

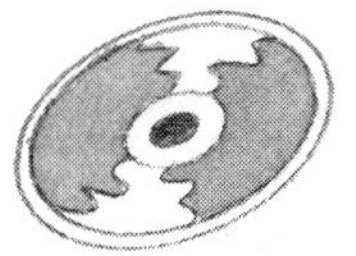

1

Hero Dogs

Dogs are everywhere! They're in parks and on the sidewalks. They're riding in cars and snoozing in the sun. Dogs are the most popular pet on the planet. In fact, they're the first animals that people ever tamed.

Scientists have found both human and dog fossils buried together in Iran, Iraq, and Israel. The fossils tell us that as long as 14,000 years ago, people and dogs lived together.

Did you know that dogs are part of the wolf family? They come from gray wolves that roamed Europe and Asia thousands of years ago. It's believed that some of the wolves began living near people. Slowly, over many years, these wolves *evolved*, or changed, into dogs.

Even today dogs are just another kind of wolf. It seems incredible that a huge Saint Bernard and a tiny Chihuahua (chee-wah-wah) share the same wolf ancestors.

Once there were many thousands of gray wolves. Over the years, people destroyed much of their habitat. And because wolves ate livestock, farmers and ranchers often killed them.

Today, gray wolves are an endangered species. But as you read this, over 400 million dogs are wagging their tails all over the world.

The scientific names for wolves and dogs are almost the same. For wolves it's Canis lupus. Dogs are Canis lupus familiaris.

Are Dogs Still Like Wolves?

In many ways, dogs and wolves are alike. They both have really amazing senses of hearing and smell. Certain dogs such as malamutes and huskies even look like wolves.

Dogs and wolves make many of the same sounds. They both howl. Wolves howl before they hunt. They howl when greeting one another. They howl to let other wolves know where they are. Dogs don't howl a lot. They usually do so only if they're upset.

Dogs and wolves each have forty-two teeth. (People usually have only thirty-two.)

Wolves and dogs growl, whimper, bark, or whine to show their feelings. Wolves don't bark as much as dogs. A wolf's bark sounds like a *chuff* rather than a full-blown bark.

Wolves and dogs are *social* animals. Wolves live in family groups called *packs* with six to ten other wolves. Dogs like to be around other dogs and with people. In a way, a dog's human family is its pack.

Social means that an animal lives with others. Elephants and dolphins are social animals. Leopards are not.

Dog and wolf mothers are protective and treat their young in similar ways. They bat, cuff, or growl at them to make them obey. If the pups really misbehave, they get a good shake or even a nip. Sometimes dog and wolf mothers stare sternly at a misbehaving pup. (Has your mother ever done that to you?)

How Dogs Are Dogs

Because dogs have been with us for so long, they can read our body language. If you point to the car or a food bowl or pick up a leash, your dog usually knows just what you mean. Without training, no other animals, even chimpanzees, are as good at this as dogs. Most dogs want to please the humans they live with.

You don't have to teach a dog to play!

This special understanding is why the bond between dogs and humans is so strong. A 14,000-year-old grave in Israel has the skeleton of a woman in it. Her hand rests on a puppy lying beside her. Even then, people loved their dogs.

Early Dogs

Because early humans hunted wild animals for food, they moved around a lot. Slowly, people began to settle down and live in small communities. They grew crops and kept livestock for food.

Dogs were important for everyone's survival. They barked when wild beasts or strangers came near. They guarded flocks, herded animals, and tracked bison and other game. They pulled carts and carried loads on their backs. Dogs also kept

A dog's body temperature is several degrees warmer than a human's.

communities cleaner by eating leftover bones and rotting meat. On cold nights, they slept with their owners and kept them nice and warm. Some folks wonder if humans could have made any progress at all without dogs.

About 12,000 years ago, people and their dogs crossed a land bridge over the Bering Strait from Siberia into Alaska.

When they reached Alaska, they became the first humans and dogs to live in North America.

Dog Breeds

As people needed dogs for certain skills such as hunting, herding, or guarding, they started *breeding* them for special purposes. Dogs in each breed began to look and act

much alike. For example, German shepherds are usually large, strong dogs with tan and black coats. This breed was created in Germany in 1899 to herd and protect sheep. These same skills make German shepherds the great police and rescue dogs they are today.

This German shepherd is training for an important job.

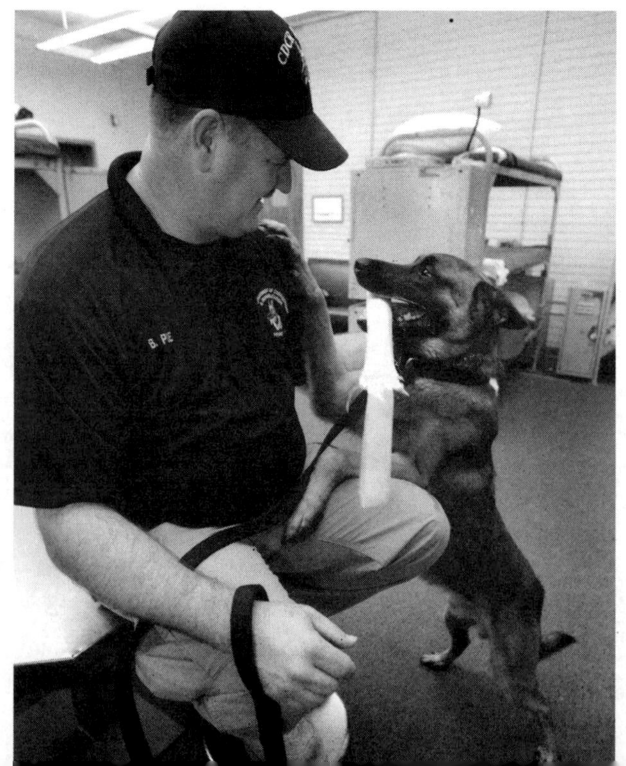

German sheeppoodle family

Among the oldest breeds in the world are the greyhound, Siberian husky, shar-pei, Pekingese, and saluki. It wasn't until the 1800s that people started to keep records of all the different breeds. They also began creating many new ones. Today there are over four hundred and the number is growing. There are also millions of dogs that are mixed breeds. Some people call these dogs mutts. Their owners often claim that mutts are the best dogs of all.

Dogs and Their Relatives

The wolf family has lots of members.

coyote
jackal
fox
African
wild dog
dingo
dog

SEARCH
DOG

2

Search and Rescue Dogs

In 2007, a Boy Scout got lost in the mountains of North Carolina. People on foot and in helicopters looked everywhere for him. On the fourth day, he was still missing. A search and rescue (SAR) dog named Gandalf and his handler arrived to help.

Gandalf's handler gave him a good whiff of the lost boy's shirt. The dog sniffed it for a long time. Finally Gandalf put his nose to the ground and took off. It wasn't long before he'd picked up the boy's scent.

After tracking him for a while, Gandalf jerked up his head and barked. This was a signal that the boy was nearby. Suddenly someone spotted him lying huddled beside the trail. The lost scout was alive.

How did Gandalf find the boy after four days? He did it with his great dog nose! Humans get most of their information from their eyes. Dogs get it from their noses. They can smell a thousand times better than humans!

Great Noses

Have you ever wondered why dogs sniff *everything*? Their constant sniffing stirs up hundreds of smells. Forty percent of their brainpower is used just for figuring out what they're smelling. Millions of *scent receptors*, or scent cells, lie inside their noses.

When dogs inhale, the smells go to these receptors. Then the receptors send information to their brains.

Dogs get more information from their sense of smell than from their eyesight. They form a sort of mental picture based on what they smell. Dogs are so good at smelling that they can pick out a single odor even when it's mixed with hundreds of others.

To use their Jacobson's organ, dogs often hold their mouths open when they smell something.

Like reptiles and many other animals, dogs have an organ on the roof of their mouth called a *Jacobson's organ.* This organ actually allows them to "taste" smells.

Dogs can track a scent even if it's several days old. They can smell things deep underground. They can smell a body underwater. They can smell things up to a mile away!

SAR Dogs

SAR dogs search for victims of avalanches, earthquakes, hurricanes, and other disasters. Every human has his or her own smell. When people move around, their skin cells flake off and drift to the ground.

Gandalf is a *tracking* dog. SAR dogs like Gandalf are trained to track a scent left on the ground by a person's skin cells. By sniffing the Boy Scout's shirt, Gandalf knew how the boy smelled. He found him by tracking the boy's scent.

Some dogs are trained to be both air-scenting and tracking dogs.

Other SAR dogs are *air-scenting* dogs. They hold their heads up to catch a human scent floating in the air. These dogs work best in parks and open fields.

Some SAR dogs are specially trained to rescue people in avalanches. Others

This SAR dog sniffs out a trail in Arizona.

are water search dogs that work in boats or along the shore to find drowning victims.

Nick Carter, Dog Detective

Nick Carter was a great dog! He was a bloodhound that lived in Kentucky in the early 1900s. Nick and his owner, Captain G. V. Mullikin, worked for the police department.

Nick Carter's job was to find missing people and criminals on the run.

Bloodhounds are an old breed. For centuries, they've been famous for their tracking ability. Bloodhounds have close to 300 million scent receptors. That's more than almost any other dog.

Don't try to sleep in the
same room with a bloodhound.
They snore very loudly!

Nick Carter was an expert tracker. He was famous for nabbing people on the run from the law. Nick never gave up, and once followed a trail more than four days old. During his career, he helped capture over six hundred criminals. Nick is known as the greatest dog detective of all time!

Heroes in the Alps

The Great Saint Bernard Pass is a fifty-mile-long road in the Swiss Alps that links Switzerland to Italy. Today the pass is a modern road and tunnel. For centuries, however, it was just a rough trail.

During the winter, icy winds and snow batter the area. The snow can be over thirty-three feet deep. In the past, travelers often froze to death, got lost or trapped in deep snow, or were buried by avalanches.

The dogs are named Saint Bernards after the monk who started the monastery in 1049.

Saint Bernards are usually close to three feet tall at their shoulders and weigh up to 200 pounds.

For years, a group of monks and their Saint Bernard dogs lived in a monastery near the pass. They rescued many people from certain death. The monks chose Saint Bernards because of their size, strength, and gentleness. Their thick fur coats made it possible for them to work in very cold weather.

The monks trained the dogs to work in teams of three without people. The big dogs plowed paths through the deep snow as they walked. Their amazing senses of smell and hearing helped them locate many travelers who were in trouble.

When they discovered someone, one of the dogs would race back to the monastery for help. The other two dogs used their big paws as shovels to dig the person out of the snow. Then they gently licked the victim's face to wake him up.

Finally the dogs would lie down on top of the stranded traveler until the monks arrived. Their huge furry bodies were much better than blankets. It's hard to freeze to death when a Saint Bernard is on top of you!

Monks and their dogs rush a man to safety.

Barry

Barry was the most famous Saint Bernard ever. He lived at the monastery in the early 1800s. Barry was fearless. He often ventured

out late at night during terrible storms to search for people. Barry saved over forty lives. After he died in 1814, the monks honored this great dog by always naming the bravest of their dogs Barry.

Now rescue teams use helicopters to search for people. Only a few monks remain at the Great Saint Bernard Pass. Their dogs have all gone to live with families. But every summer, a few return to welcome visitors who come to see the famous dogs of the Saint Bernard Pass.

Some avalanche rescue equipment today is called Barryvox, which means "Barry's voice," in honor of Barry.

Hunter in Haiti

On January 12, 2010, Haiti had a horrendous earthquake. Buildings collapsed, trapping many people underneath. Dog rescue teams raced to Haiti from the United States.

Los Angeles firefighter Bill Monahan was on the scene with his border collie, Hunter. Four days after the quake, Hunter and Bill were still crisscrossing the ruins. It seemed impossible that anyone remained alive, but they hadn't given up. Hunter went back and forth over the piles of concrete. Suddenly he gave his *alert* bark.

Hunter had found three girls trapped under four feet of twisted steel and concrete! They were still alive! Bill quickly passed water bottles down to them. One of the girls whispered, "Thank you." Because of Hunter and Bill, the girls survived.

German shepherds, Labradors, and border collies often make good SAR dogs. But SAR dogs do not have to be a certain breed. They just have to be smart, strong, and hardworking. They also have to be willing to work in all kinds of weather and under all kinds of conditions. SAR dogs are very tough dogs.

Hunter and Bill share a loving moment during the earthquake rescue.

Training Search and Rescue Dogs

It takes about six hundred hours to train SAR dogs. Here are just a few things besides tracking skills that they learn to do:

- Obey basic commands like *come*, *sit*, *stay*, and *heel*.
- Focus while walking on a loose leash, even when there are noises, passing joggers, or other distractions.
- Obey for a long time when told to sit, no matter what else is happening.

- Remain calm while going through tunnels, getting into tractor buckets and being lifted ten feet in the air, and going down mountains in a harness.
- Climb up steep A-frames, jump over objects, and walk across beams that might wiggle.

- Ignore other dogs and not sniff them.
- Climb rope ladders that wiggle even more than beams.

3

The Dogs of 9/11

On September 11, 2001, terrorists crashed two planes into the twin towers of the World Trade Center in New York City. The first plane hit the north tower at 8:46 a.m. Omar Rivera worked on the seventy-first floor. Omar is blind. He was at his computer with his guide dog, Salty, at his feet.

Suddenly Omar heard a huge booming sound. Glass shattered, fires broke out, and the building began to crack and sway. Terrified people huddled in their offices.

Omar clipped on Salty's leash and told him to go toward the stairs. As they started down, a second plane hit the south tower at 9:03.

Because of the thick smoke and dust, it was hard to breathe. Salty never gave up. As the two struggled down the stairs, firefighters rushed up past them. Broken glass

Omar and Salty are at an award ceremony to honor dogs of 9/11.

and chunks of concrete made walking difficult. Salty led Omar slowly and safely around all the obstacles.

It took almost an hour for the two to reach the lobby. By then the south tower had collapsed. Once outside, fumes from burning jet fuel seared their throats and eyes. At 10:28 another unearthly roar shook the ground. The north tower had fallen as well.

Mountains of dust and debris shot hundreds of feet into the sky, blotting out the sun. The ash-covered survivors looked like ghosts as they staggered down the sidewalks. Nearly 3,000 people lay dead under millions of tons of rubble. But thanks to Salty, Omar was not one of them. The site where the once-proud towers had stood was now nothing but huge piles of smoking ruins.

Among the dead were 343 firefighters and paramedics and 23 police officers.

There were about 108 million tons of wreckage at Ground Zero.

Dogs on the Scene

Rescue teams from all over the country rushed to New York City. Over four hundred

SAR dogs and their handlers arrived as well. It was the largest dog rescue mission in history.

Officer Scott Ryan, a New York City policeman, and his dog, Taz, were among the first on the scene. Taz was a member of the NYPD *K-9 dog* unit. Later, Scott said he and Taz had the utmost trust in each other. He also said that Taz was the best partner he'd ever had.

K-9 dogs help police find suspects as well as drugs, missing people, and explosives.

Mary Flood and her black Lab, Jake, came from Utah. Mary had adopted Jake when he was an injured puppy. She'd nursed him back to health and trained him as a SAR dog.

Everyone welcomed the dogs. Jake got a free steak dinner on his first night in town.

Janet Linker of the Seattle Fire Department brought along her rescue dog, Ricky. He was the smallest dog there. A rat terrier, Ricky stood only seventeen inches high. But he was great at squeezing into very small cracks. He could even climb metal ladders!

Dogs at Work

The dogs got down to business. Every night and day, each team worked twelve-hour shifts. Many dogs wore special vests that said "Search Dog" or "Police." Tons of rubble, broken glass, and metal were piled hundreds of feet high. Fires still smoldered under the ruins.

Fires burned under the rubble for three months.

The dogs were tireless in their efforts to find survivors. They dug, crawled on their bellies into holes, and struggled up and down the massive ruins. When workers cut new holes in the wreckage, they'd yell "Dog over here!" A dog and its handler would hurry to the spot, hopeful of finding someone alive.

Riley is lifted over one pile of wreckage to another.

Because the work was so tiring, the dogs needed to take frequent rest breaks. Veterinarians set up medical stations so they could treat them for cuts, dehydration,

Chiropractors gave the dogs free massages to ease their sore muscles.

and exhaustion. Many wore special dog boots to protect their paws.

A dog named Bear takes a break from his work at Ground Zero.

Dogs as Healers

On the second day, Trakr, a German shepherd, found the last survivor. He and his handler had come all the way from

Canada. Trakr was a police dog trained to catch criminals and find missing people. All of his training paid off. Trakr located a woman who had been trapped in the wreckage for twenty-six hours.

After a week, there was no hope of finding anyone else alive. Everyone was exhausted. Many workers sought comfort from the dogs. They smiled when a dog dropped a ball at their feet. They napped with the dogs and played with them. Some just sat and held them.

Tests show that dogs help people feel less stress.

The dogs were also under stress. Most were trained to rescue survivors. Now there were only dead bodies or nothing at all to find. Their handlers tried to cheer the dogs up by hiding behind concrete beams and trucks so the dogs could "find" someone and get a reward. Somehow, everybody just kept going.

The Job Ends

It was finally over. After many days on the job, Jake, Ricky, Taz, Trakr, and all the other dogs went home. Jake had worked for seventeen days. In 2005, he had another tough job searching for victims of Hurricane Katrina. Janet took little Ricky back to Washington. He'd found several people before he left. Taz and Scott returned to police work. Before Trakr's owner took him home, Trakr had to be treated for exhaustion and for breathing in smoke. Scott later said, "All the dogs—they all knew what we wanted them to do, and they did it."

Turn the page to find out about another famous dog of 9/11.

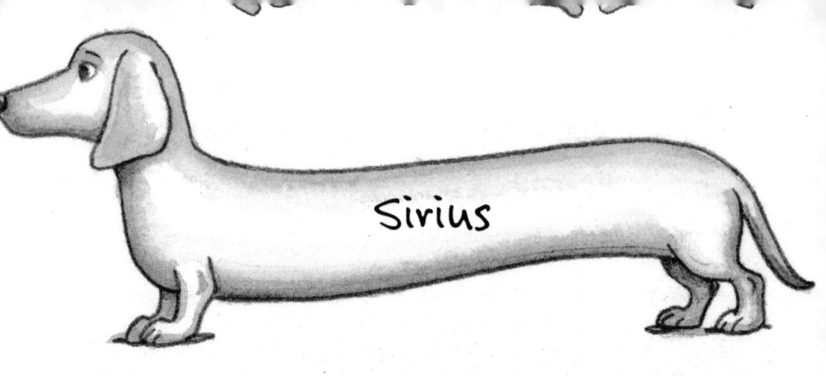

Sirius was a bomb-sniffing dog on duty at the World Trade Center on September 11. Police Sergeant David Lim, his partner, was with him in their basement office.

When the first plane struck, David put Sirius in his kennel to keep him safe and rushed to help. David was in the south tower when it collapsed. He, six firefighters, and an injured woman were buried for five hours. Finally they were rescued.

Sadly, Sirius was not so lucky. He was the only dog that died when the towers fell. David Lim was heartbroken about his friend. Over four hundred people and K-9 teams from all over the country came to Sirius's memorial service. Today a special dog run in a park near Ground Zero is named in Sirius's honor.

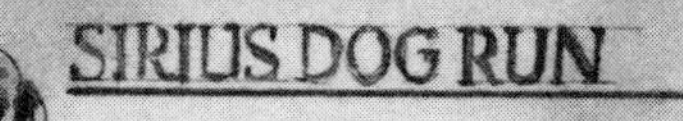

4

Service Dogs

Life is hard for people who cannot see, hear, or walk well. It's also difficult for people with certain diseases. Service dogs can often help. Their job is to help keep disabled people alive and well.

A number of service dogs come from animal shelters.

Trainers choose service dogs by picking out puppies that are social, obedient, and healthy. They also select puppies that learn quickly and are calm. Labs, shepherds, and golden retrievers often make good service dogs.

Trainers make sure the puppies are relaxed around people. They expose them to

Service dogs can do many of these things:

Guide blind people across busy streets.

Alert deaf people to noises from doorbells, telephones, and crying babies.

children, noisy streets, and busy crowds. The dogs first learn the basics, such as how

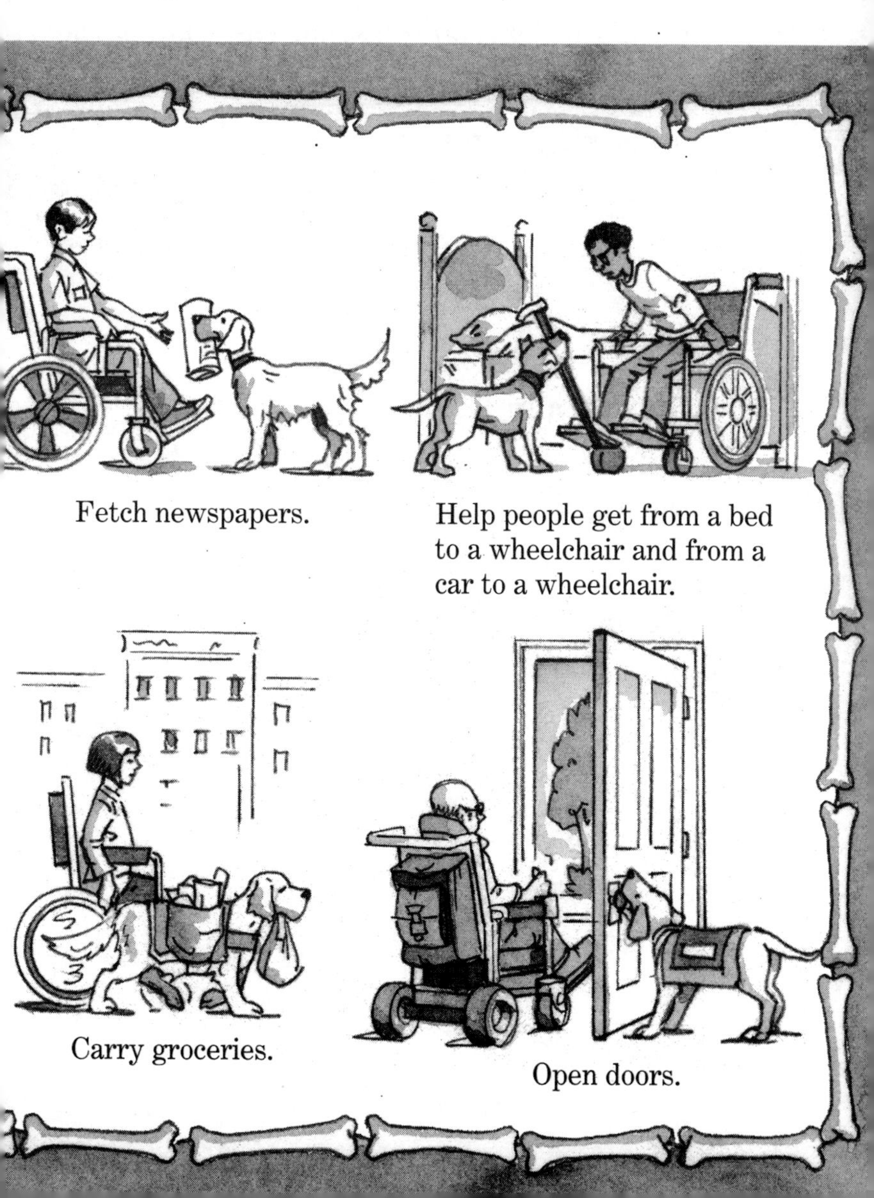

Fetch newspapers.

Help people get from a bed to a wheelchair and from a car to a wheelchair.

Carry groceries.

Open doors.

to walk on leashes, obey simple commands, and stay focused *no matter what*! Then they learn special skills, such as guiding the blind or helping people who have lost the use of their arms or legs.

Today there are over 15,000 service dogs living with disabled people in the United States and Canada.

Shirley and Rebecca

Wherever Rebecca Farrar goes, her dog, Shirley, goes, too. Shirley is not just a pet. She keeps Rebecca alive. Rebecca is an English schoolgirl with a disease called *diabetes*.

If Rebecca's blood sugar level gets too low or too high, she might slip into a coma. She might even die. Rebecca tests her blood many times a day. When there is a change, she takes a medicine called *insulin*.

Shirley wears a yellow medical alert dog bib when she's on the job.

Rebecca can't always tell when she needs insulin, but Shirley can. She is a *hypo-alert* dog. Hypo-alert dogs are trained to smell changes in people's blood sugar levels. There are only a few other dogs like Shirley in Great Britain.

Shirley can smell when Rebecca's blood sugar levels change. When this happens, she licks Rebecca's hand to alert her. Sometimes she'll even bring a blood sugar testing kit to her.

Before she had Shirley, Rebecca had to go to the hospital three or four times a week. Now she can relax because Shirley is on the job. No wonder Rebecca says Shirley is her best friend!

Buddy and Morris

In 1927, Morris Frank was a blind college student in Tennessee. At that time, there were no guide dogs in the United States. Morris needed help getting around.

Morris and Buddy

Morris heard about a woman in Switzerland who trained German shepherds as guide dogs. Her name was Dorothy Eustis. Morris traveled to Switzerland to meet her. Dorothy introduced him to a guide dog named Buddy.

Morris began working with Buddy. When they walked, Morris held on to a harness that Buddy wore. He learned to

give her clear commands such as *forward*, *right*, and *left*. If something was blocking the way, Buddy led Morris around it. Morris began to trust her completely.

When Morris and Buddy arrived home, reporters raced to see the first guide dog in the country. The noisy mob followed as Buddy led Morris down the crowded city sidewalks.

Morris later said he could hear trucks whizzing by in the streets, cabs blowing their horns, and people shouting at them.

When Buddy saw it was safe to walk, she led Morris across the street. Once they got to the other side, Morris gave her a big hug.

Morris Frank and Dorothy Eustis started a guide dog school in the United States in 1929. They called it The Seeing Eye. Since then, it has trained thousands of dogs. The school is so famous that many people call all guide dogs Seeing Eye dogs.

But today many other schools also train dogs for the blind. Thousands of blind people in Canada and the United States have guide dogs that act as eyes for their owners.

Some of the most popular guide dogs are Labrador retrievers.

Roland and Rainbow

Many soldiers have returned from wars with terrible injuries. Some have lost legs or arms.

After Roland Paquette was injured in Afghanistan in 2004, he really needed help. Roland lost both legs due to an explosion. He was fitted with artificial legs but sometimes needed a wheelchair. He also needed a dog named Rainbow.

Some service dogs can dial 911 in emergencies!

Rainbow was the first service dog given to a soldier who used both artificial legs and a wheelchair. Rainbow helps Roland keep his balance while he walks. After Roland takes the legs off at night, Rainbow picks things up off the floor or gets them from shelves and tabletops for him.

It takes about two years and a lot of money to train a good service dog. All over the world, people with disabilities rely on service dogs just like Shirley, Buddy, and Rainbow for help and comfort.

Rainbow can even turn lights on and off for Roland.

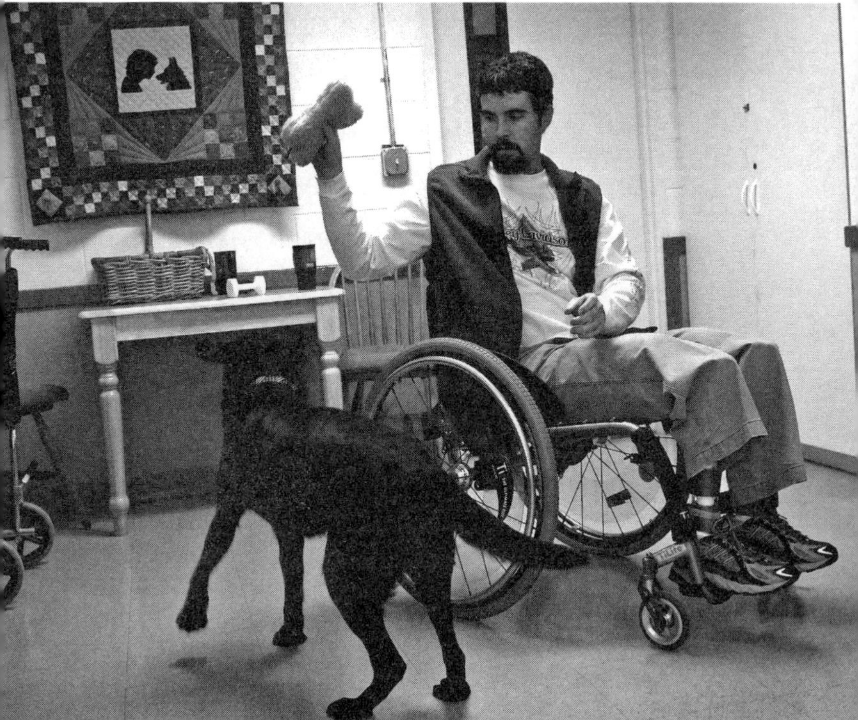

Therapy Dogs

Dogs can be great medicine! Therapy dogs work in hospitals, nursing homes, and prisons to comfort people. Max is a Great Dane . . . a really *big* Great Dane. Standing on his hind legs, he's six feet and two inches tall! He and his owner often visit sick children at Miami Children's Hospital.

Like doctors and nurses, Max wears his own identification card. It says "Pet Therapy, Max." All the kids love him. Max loves all the kids. They hug him and get big sloppy kisses in return. Max is gentle and patient. He always cheers the kids up and makes them laugh. Even if they pull his tail,

Max doesn't mind at all. He just wags it harder. Therapy dogs make many people smile when they haven't in a long time.

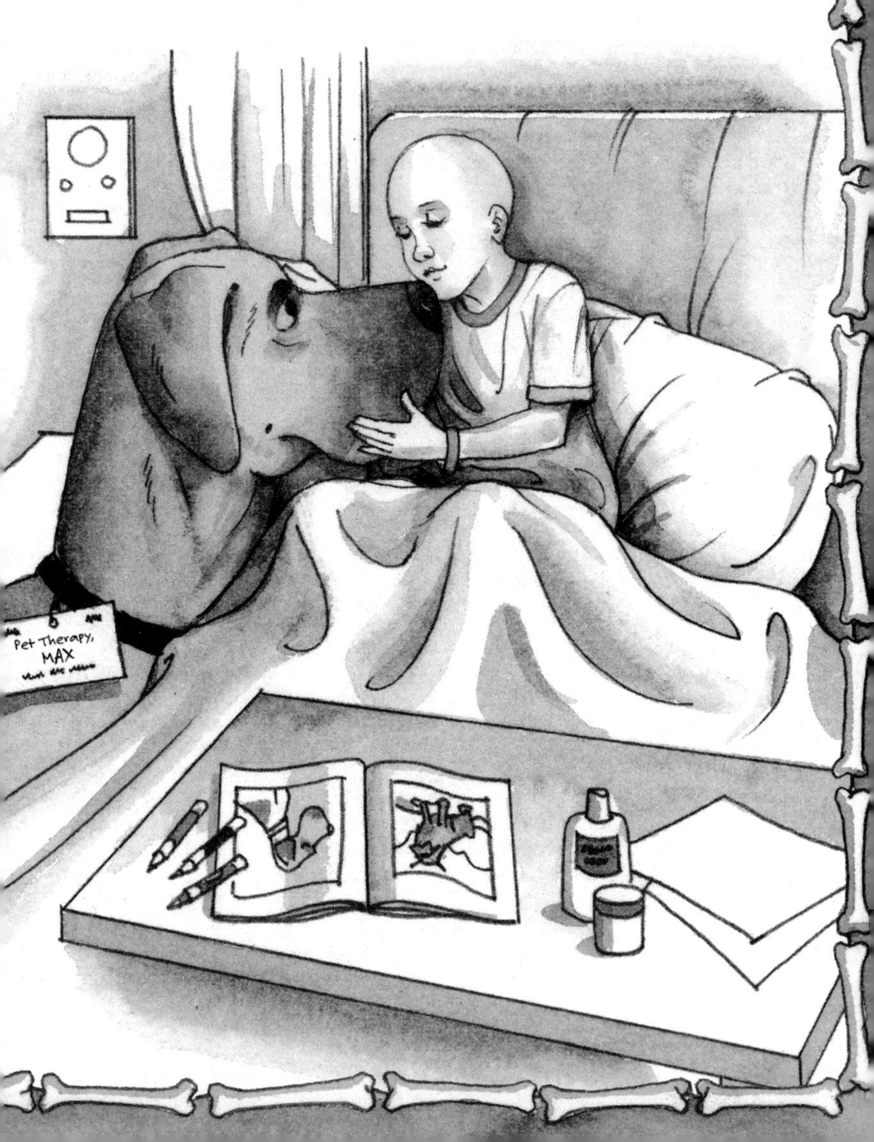

HERO
HERO
HERO

5

Famous Dog Heroes

SAR and service dogs train for emergencies all the time. These dogs often do very brave things, especially when they work with soldiers. Thousands of dogs have proven their bravery in times of war. One of them was named Stubby. In 1918, when the United States fought in World War I, Stubby went into battle with the soldiers over seventeen times. He once caught a German spy and dragged him out by the seat of his pants! After the war, Stubby was invited to the White House twice.

Stubby was the most decorated dog of World War I.

But what about ordinary dogs . . . like the one sleeping on your couch or barking at nothing at all in the backyard? Time after time, ordinary dogs with no training save people from fires, drag them from wrecked cars, and warn them of danger.

Some researchers say that all dogs sense danger faster than humans. They seem to have a sixth sense about when they need to protect people or when something is going to happen.

In Kenya, a stray mother dog found a baby in a forest. The dog's own litter of puppies was on the other side of a busy road. She managed to carry the baby across the road to her puppies, where someone discovered her. The baby lived—thanks to the efforts of a protective mother dog.

Then there is HJ, who ran for help when his owner, a farmer, had a heart attack. HJ raced off to get the farmer's wife. When he found her, he nudged her arm until she went to check on her husband. HJ is now in the Iowa Animal Hall of Fame. His owner says they've petted him so much, he's losing his hair!

In Australia, a dog named Levi stopped his owner from rushing back into her burning house to turn off the electricity.

The stories about all of these dogs, trained and untrained, are endless. Every day some new story appears about a dog that has done something unbelievable. Maybe yours will, too!

Now let's track down some really great dog heroes!

Balto

In January 1925, Nome, Alaska, was hit by an outbreak of *diphtheria* (diff-THEER-ee-uh). This disease was especially hard on children. The nearest medicine was a thousand miles away in Anchorage. Because of subzero temperatures, the only airplane had a frozen engine. Cars were stuck, too. Medicine was sent by train to Nenana, about six hundred miles from Nome. Twenty dog teams stood by in relay teams to deliver it.

Gunnar Kaasen volunteered to do the last leg of the trip with his thirteen dogs.

He'd chosen Balto as the lead dog. Balto was a big black Siberian husky with a white patch shaped like a heart on his chest.

A raging blizzard battered the team. At times Gunnar couldn't see his hands in front of his face. But Balto never once got confused. He stayed on the trail no matter what. Once when he refused to move, Gunnar discovered that they were headed toward a river. At last the team arrived in Nome, exhausted and weak. Thanks to Balto and all the other great dog teams, the medicine arrived just in time.

Buddy

Buddy lives with his owner, Ben, on a country road in Alaska. One day a fire broke out in Ben's workshop. Ben fought the fire until he burned his hands. The fire was threatening his house! Ben shouted for Buddy to get help.

The big German shepherd took off like a shot. Meanwhile, neighbors had called 911. A highway patrol officer tried to speed to the scene, but he got confused on the back roads. Suddenly he spotted Buddy. Buddy turned around in front of his car and headed

for home. Somehow the patrolman knew he should follow. His dashboard camera caught Buddy in action. It shows the big dog streaking down the road. At times he looks back to make sure the car is still there.

After they reached the house, firemen arrived to put out the blaze. The shop was a total loss, but Ben's house was saved. Alaska state troopers had a ceremony to honor Buddy. They rewarded him with a big rawhide bone. He also got a dog bowl with the words *diligence and assistance* engraved on it.

Chips

Chips may have been the bravest dog in World War II. Early one morning, Chips and his handler, John Rowell, were with troops on a beach in Sicily. Enemy gunfire broke out. The soldiers were pinned down and couldn't move. Suddenly Chips broke away from John. Trailing his leash, he rushed directly to the spot where Italian gunners were firing.

In an instant, Chips dragged one of the men out of his hiding place. Three other men followed with their hands up in the air. During the fight, Chips received some gunpowder burns and a cut on his head.

Later that night, Chips alerted soldiers to more enemy action. Ten other prisoners were captured.

Chips stayed in the war for three years.

During that time, he often went into battle with his unit. Before Chips returned home in 1945, the soldiers gave him a special medal to honor his bravery.

Shana

Eve and Norman Fertig run an animal sanctuary in New York. One night they were in one of the buildings feeding animals. It had been a nice fall day, but a blizzard with gale-force winds suddenly blew in. When the lights went out, Norman and Eve left the building to see why. Just then a massive tree fell. It completely blocked their way. They couldn't reach any shelter at all and huddled together for warmth. Things looked bad.

Shana, an adopted hybrid wolf dog, stayed with them constantly. She began digging under the fallen tree. Shana was making a tunnel! She dug with all her might, using her paws and even her mouth to clear the way. At times, she barked as if to tell them to follow her. Shana tunneled all the way to the house. It took her almost three hours!

Because the tunnel wasn't very large, Eve had to lie down to get through it while Shana dragged her by her sleeve. Then Norman grabbed Eve's legs and Shana pulled them both. Finally they all stumbled into the house. Since the electricity was off, the house was very cold. Shana lay on top of them and kept them warm until help arrived the next morning.

Bo

Laurie and Bob Roberts were rafting down the Colorado River. The couple had their Labrador retriever, Bo, and a new puppy named Duchess with them.

Everyone was having fun until an eight-foot wave hit the raft. The raft flipped over, and Bob and Duchess were thrown clear. But Bo and Laurie were trapped underneath in the raging water. Somehow Bo managed to swim free. Laurie was still trapped and in danger of drowning!

Bo turned around and swam back down under the raft. As Bob looked on helplessly, Bo appeared once more. This time he was dragging Laurie by the hair! She managed to grab on to Bo's big tail. He pulled her through the strong current back to the shore.

Like most Labs, Bo is a great swimmer. Labs have webbed feet and powerful tails that propel them easily through the water. Thanks to Bo, these things really helped Laurie, too!

6

Just Call a Dog!

When geese land on golf courses, parks, and lakes, each one produces about a pound of waste a day! Their droppings are unhealthy and annoying. Geese were polluting the University of Washington's fountains and grounds. Things were getting messy—*really* messy.

Officials asked Tom Finnelly and his dog, Jerry, for help. They needed them to go on goose patrol. Tom had trained Jerry to chase geese away from public places. Jerry doesn't hurt the geese; he just scares them. Since Jerry's been on patrol, the grass and fountains are much cleaner and safer!

All over the country, cities and towns are hiring dogs to do what Jerry does. Dogs can actually do many different jobs. If you need something done, just call a dog. Some of them might amaze you.

Wildlife Detector Dogs

There are some dogs that help *ecologists.* Ecologists study living things and their environment. Dave Vesely is a wildlife biologist and ecologist in Oregon. Dave keeps track of endangered western pond turtles. Because the turtles cover their nests with grass and dirt, he often had a hard time finding their eggs.

Dave and Chilko search for turtle nests.

Dave owned a Belgian sheepdog named Chilko. He trained the dog to sniff out turtle nests. Chilko became an expert western pond turtle nest tracker!

Dave also taught Rogue, his other Belgian sheepdog, to locate a rare plant called Kincaid's lupine. An endangered butterfly depends on the lupine for food. In order to protect the butterflies' habitat, Dave needed to know where the lupine grew. Rogue is now a fabulous lupine finder! When Rogue does a good job, Dave rewards him with a doggie treat. "We have a big party every time he finds one," Dave said.

Other dogs help wildlife researchers find animal feces, or *scat.* Scat reveals what species an animal is, whether it is male or female, and what kind of food it has eaten. This helps researchers keep track of all the animals in an area.

Some dogs are especially good at finding scat floating in water. Standing on the bow of a boat, they sniff for the location of Atlantic right whales and orcas. The dogs can smell their scat over a mile away! Researchers say they are always 100 percent correct.

This dog leads the way to orcas!

A dog named Sable detects sewage and other pollutants in water.

A dog named Tammy searches fishing boats in South Africa for illegal catches of abalone, an endangered shellfish. Trained dogs in Nevada find desert tortoises. Some dogs have even traced ivory poached from African elephants. Soon dogs are going to set up research labs! (Just kidding, but you never know.)

R.E.A.D. Dogs

R.E.A.D. dogs are special dogs trained to sit with children as they read. They are also trained to look at the reader. Some of the dogs even turn pages. Many children say they can relax reading to dogs and don't feel shy or scared. A lot of students have noticed that their reading grades have gone up. Maybe it just takes a reading dog to help some kids get to love books!

Kids say the R.E.A.D. dogs never make fun of them if they don't know a word.

Bomb Sniffers

In 2009, Lance Leddy was a marine stationed in Afghanistan. Lance's partner was a bomb-sniffing Labrador retriever named Lode. They were one of thirteen bomb-detecting teams in Lance's unit. Terrorists often placed bombs on the roads in Afghanistan to blow up military trucks and tanks. Lance and Lode worked closely together to find the bombs. Dogs can often find explosives that metal detectors miss.

Sniffer dogs also detect explosives and drugs at airports, train stations, and border crossings.

Like all bomb-sniffing dogs, Lode obeyed a series of whistles and arm signals. He was trained to be alert for piles of gravel or boxes on the road. Lance said that when it was time to go home, he really missed Lode. "I've owned a few dogs," he said, "but nothing like this. I mean, these dogs are amazing."

Dogs Save Cheetahs

Because cheetahs attack livestock, farmers in South Africa killed them in great numbers. Wildlife experts were afraid that cheetahs would disappear altogether.

Peter Knipe owns a farm there. He has goats, cattle, impalas, and even giraffes. Peter had cheetah problems. But in 2008, he brought an Anatolian shepherd over from Turkey. Anatolian

Anatolians are not great pets. They're very independent and strong-willed.

shepherds have a 6,000-year history of protecting goats and sheep on farms there.

Peter's dog, Neeake, spent his puppy days guarding goats. Now he guards Peter's animals. When Neeake spots cheetahs or other predators, he charges toward them, barking fiercely. Since Neeake has been on duty, there have been no cheetah attacks. Other farmers are using Anatolian shepherds as well. The results are safe cheetahs and safe livestock. Everyone is a winner!

Bilbo the Lifeguard

People at Sennen Beach in England were really upset. Bilbo had been banned! Bilbo was the only official lifeguard dog in the country. For two years, he'd worked with his owner and fellow lifeguard, Steve Jamieson. Steve trained him to swim out in rough seas with a life buoy to pull people to safety.

Bilbo reports for duty!

Once when a woman ignored warnings of dangerous currents, Bilbo tried to block her path. When she went in anyway, he swam in front of her to protect her.

Now there was a new rule: no more dogs on the beach, even Bilbo! Ten thousand people signed petitions demanding his return. Finally officials let Bilbo go back to work. Everyone cheered!

Many More Jobs

Dogs do other interesting jobs. Some can detect insects that might be bad for crops or deadly mold growing under houses. Medical researchers are working with dogs to see if they can smell cancer in people. There seems to be no end of things for dogs to do. Maybe you can even train your dog to make your bed!

This beagle sniffs out termites that could eat away at people's homes.

Dog as King

There is a legend that a dog was once king of Norway. The saga began during the rule of King Eystein over eight hundred years ago. He got very angry at his people. To punish them, the king gave them a choice. They could have either his dog, Saur, or his slave as their king for three years. The people chose Saur.

Myth has it that Saur had the wisdom of three men. It was also said that every three or four noises he made came out as words. Saur was supposed to have worn a beautiful gold collar and sat on a high throne. When he went out, servants carried him on their shoulders. Stories even tell about how Saur stamped his paw prints on every official document!

7

Dogs as Thinking Animals

Dogs seem to have deep feelings for their human families. Some are quiet and don't eat when their owners are away. Some mourn for months when their owners die.

Scientists used to think that dogs behaved this way only because of *instinct*. But now researchers are finding that instinct alone doesn't explain everything.

Instinct is when an animal acts automatically without thinking.

Professor Marc Bekoff is an expert on

animal behavior. His research has shown that dogs are thinking animals with true emotions. They feel love. They seem to know right from wrong. Professor Bekoff says the bond between dogs and humans is deeper than anyone has ever imagined.

While dogs are not human, they do some very human things. For example, dogs laugh by panting in quick, even breaths. They try to sneak food *very* quietly if they think someone might hear. Dogs even have a sense of fair play with other dogs and have their own set of doggie rules. Stray dogs in Moscow have learned to ride the subways and get off when they want to. They've also been spotted obeying traffic lights!

Dogs continue to comfort and inspire us. They are our strongest link to the animal kingdom. Dogs remind us that we, too, are social animals who depend on our animal senses to survive. Maybe it doesn't matter so much what dogs really understand about us. Just being with a loving dog is good enough.

Doing More Research

There's a lot more you can learn about dog heroes. The fun of research is seeing how many different sources you can explore.

Books

Most libraries and bookstores have books about heroic dogs.

Here are some things to remember when you're using books for research:

1. You don't have to read the whole book. Check the table of contents and the index to find the topics you're interested in.

2. Write down the name of the book.

When you take notes, make sure you write down the name of the book in your notebook so you can find it again.

3. Never copy exactly from a book.

When you learn something new from a book, put it in your own words.

4. Make sure the book is nonfiction.

Some books tell make-believe stories about dog heroes. Make-believe stories are called *fiction.* They're fun to read, but not good for research.

Research books have facts and tell true stories. They are called *nonfiction.* A librarian or teacher can help you make sure the books you use for research are nonfiction.

Here are some good nonfiction books about dog heroes:

- *Animal Rescuers* by Rosanna Hansen
- *Buddy: The First Seeing Eye Dog* by Eva Moore
- *Dog Heroes*, A Story Poster Book, by Karl Meyer
- *Hero Dogs: 100 True Stories of Daring Deeds* by Peter C. Jones and Lisa MacDonald
- *Hero Dogs: Courageous Canines in Action* by Donna M. Jackson
- *Service Dogs*, Dog Heroes series, by Linda Tagliaferro
- *War Dog Heroes: True Stories of Dog Courage in Wartime* by Jeannette Sanderson

Museums and Zoos

Many museums have exhibits about dogs, dog and wolf evolution, and dog heroes. Some zoos have wolves. These places can help you learn more about dogs and wolves.

When you go to a museum or zoo:

1. Be sure to take your notebook!

Write down anything that catches your interest. Draw pictures, too!

2. Ask questions.

There are almost always people at museums and zoos who can help you find what you're looking for.

3. Check the calendar.

Many museums and zoos have special events and activities just for kids!

Here are some museums and zoos that have exhibits about dogs and wolves:

- American Museum of Natural History (New York)
- Cleveland Museum of Natural History
- March Field Air Museum (Riverside, California)
- National Zoo (Washington, D.C.)
- San Diego Zoo

DVDs

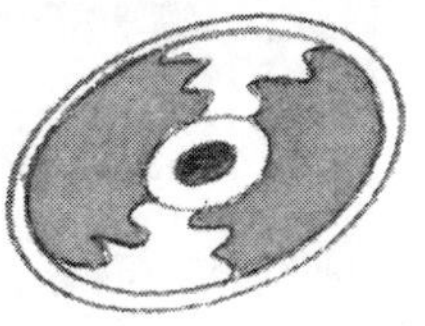

There are some great nonfiction DVDs about dogs, wolves, and dog heroes. As with books, make sure the DVDs you watch for research are nonfiction!

Check your library or video store for these and other nonfiction titles about dogs and wolves:

- *And Man Created Dog*
  from National Geographic
- *Dogs and More Dogs*
  from NOVA
- *Dogs Decoded*
  from NOVA
- *A Man Among Wolves*
  from National Geographic
- Nature: *Dogs that Changed the World*
  from Questar

The Internet

Many websites have facts about dogs and dog heroes. Some also have games and activities that can help make learning about dogs even more fun.

Ask your teacher or your parents to help you find more websites like these:

- animal.discovery.com/tv/dogs-101
- dogguide.net/25-hero-dogs.php
- www.dogheroesof911.com/photoslide.htm
- enchantedlearning.com/subjects/mammals/dog/index.shtml
- historyforkids.org/learn/economy/dogs.htm
- news.nationalgeographic.com/news/2004/02/0209_040209_dogsdogsdogs.html

- pawnation.com/2010/03/25/dogs-heroics-earn-national-honor

Good luck!

Index

Photographs courtesy of:

© **AP Photo/David Karp** (p. 44). © **AP Photo/Beth A. Keiser** (p. 50). © **AP Photo/Rich Pedroncelli** (p. 22). © **AP Photo/Reed Saxon** (p. 39). © **BenLister.com** (p. 61). © **Bettmann/CORBIS** (p. 74). © **Ira Block/National Geographic Stock** (p. 51). © **Rob Elliott/Stringer/AFP/Getty Images** (p. 67). © **Fred Felleman** (p. 93). © **Thomas Imo/Alamy** (p. 107). **Courtesy Intermountain Therapy Animals/R.E.A.D. Program** (p. 95). © **Mike Kemp/Photolibrary** (p. 18). © **Geoffrey Kuchera, 2011. Used under license from Shutterstock.com** (p. 16 right). © **Eduard Kyslynskyy, 2011. Used under license from Shutterstock.com** (p. 16 left). © **Jean-Michel Labat/ardea.com** (cover). © **Mary Evans/Grenville Collins Postcard Collection** (p. 36). © **Steve McCurry/Magnum Photos** (p. 46). © **Andrea Mohin/*The New York Times*/Redux Pictures** (p. 69). © **Tom Nebbia/CORBIS** (p. 101). © **Jeronimo Nisa/*The Bay City Times*** (p. 94). © **Jim Parkin, 2011. Used under license from Shutterstock.com** (p. 31). © **THOMAS PATTERSON/*Statesman Journal*** (p. 91). © **George Pickow/Stringer/Getty Images** (p. 35). © **Colin Shepherd/Rex USA** (p. 99). © **M Smith/Newspix/Rex USA** (p. 76). **Courtesy of the Tennessee State Library and Archives** (p. 63). © **U.S. Navy/Handout/Getty Images** (p. 49). © **Petra Wegner/Alamy** (p. 23).

Have you read the adventure that matches up with this book?

Don't miss

Magic Tree House® Merlin Mission #18

DOGS IN THE DEAD OF NIGHT

The magic tree house whisks Jack and Annie back in time to the highest pass in the Swiss Alps, a world of avalanches and blizzards, to find a rare flower. They make it safely to an ancient monastery filled with monks and Saint Bernard dogs. Then the monks ask them to take care of a wild puppy named Barry. Can Barry help Jack and Annie find the flower? Or will he only make things worse?

Enough cool facts to fill a tree house!

Jack and Annie have been all over the world in their adventures in the magic tree house. And they've learned lots of incredible facts along the way. Now they want to share them with you! Get ready for a collection of the weirdest, grossest, funniest, most all-around amazing facts that Jack and Annie have ever encountered. It's the ultimate fact attack!

Magic Tree House®

#1: Dinosaurs Before Dark
#2: The Knight at Dawn
#3: Mummies in the Morning
#4: Pirates Past Noon
#5: Night of the Ninjas
#6: Afternoon on the Amazon
#7: Sunset of the Sabertooth
#8: Midnight on the Moon
#9: Dolphins at Daybreak
#10: Ghost Town at Sundown
#11: Lions at Lunchtime
#12: Polar Bears Past Bedtime
#13: Vacation Under the Volcano
#14: Day of the Dragon King
#15: Viking Ships at Sunrise
#16: Hour of the Olympics
#17: Tonight on the *Titanic*
#18: Buffalo Before Breakfast
#19: Tigers at Twilight
#20: Dingoes at Dinnertime
#21: Civil War on Sunday
#22: Revolutionary War on Wednesday
#23: Twister on Tuesday
#24: Earthquake in the Early Morning
#25: Stage Fright on a Summer Night
#26: Good Morning, Gorillas
#27: Thanksgiving on Thursday
#28: High Tide in Hawaii

Magic Tree House®
Merlin Missions

#1: Christmas in Camelot
#2: Haunted Castle on Hallows Eve
#3: Summer of the Sea Serpent
#4: Winter of the Ice Wizard
#5: Carnival at Candlelight
#6: Season of the Sandstorms
#7: Night of the New Magicians
#8: Blizzard of the Blue Moon
#9: Dragon of the Red Dawn
#10: Monday with a Mad Genius
#11: Dark Day in the Deep Sea
#12: Eve of the Emperor Penguin
#13: Moonlight on the Magic Flute
#14: A Good Night for Ghosts
#15: Leprechaun in Late Winter
#16: A Ghost Tale for Christmas Time
#17: A Crazy Day with Cobras
#18: Dogs in the Dead of Night
#19: Abe Lincoln at Last!
#20: A Perfect Time for Pandas
#21: Stallion by Starlight
#22: Hurry Up, Houdini!
#23: High Time for Heroes
#24: Soccer on Sunday
#25: Shadow of the Shark
#26: Balto of the Blue Dawn
#27: Night of the Ninth Dragon

Magic Tree House® Super Edition

#1: World at War, 1944

Magic Tree House® Fact Trackers

Dinosaurs
Knights and Castles
Mummies and Pyramids
Pirates
Rain Forests
Space
Titanic
Twisters and Other Terrible Storms
Dolphins and Sharks
Ancient Greece and the Olympics
American Revolution
Sabertooths and the Ice Age
Pilgrims
Ancient Rome and Pompeii
Tsunamis and Other Natural Disasters
Polar Bears and the Arctic
Sea Monsters
Penguins and Antarctica
Leonardo da Vinci
Ghosts
Leprechauns and Irish Folklore
Rags and Riches: Kids in the Time of Charles Dickens
Snakes and Other Reptiles
Dog Heroes
Abraham Lincoln
Pandas and Other Endangered Species
Horse Heroes
Heroes for All Times
Soccer
Ninjas and Samurai
China: Land of the Emperor's Great Wall
Sharks and Other Predators
Vikings
Dogsledding and Extreme Sports
Dragons and Mythical Creatures
World War II

More Magic Tree House®

Games and Puzzles from the Tree House
Magic Tricks from the Tree House
My Magic Tree House Journal
Magic Tree House Survival Guide
Animal Games and Puzzles
Magic Tree House Incredible Fact Book